60 Easy Classics

For

Clarinet

60 Classical pieces
some well known, others less so
arranged for Clarinet players
of Grade 1-4 standard
with many entirely below the break

Includes useful musical facts and information
Soundtrack available to download from our website

Amanda Oosthuizen

Jemima Oosthuizen

The Catchy Clarinet Series
Wild Music Publications
www.wildmusicpublications.com

We hope you enjoy *60 Easy Classics for Clarinet!*

We have loads more books for you,
such as: *Christmas Duets and Trios, 50+ Greatest Classics, 50+ Greatest Intermediate Classics, Clarinet Music Theory, Trick or Treat – A Halloween Suite, Easy Duets from Around the World, Moonlight and Roses, Fish 'n' Ships, Intermediate Classic Duets,*
and many more!

To see what you might be missing out on, visit:
http://WildMusicPublications.com

Happy Music-Making!

The Wild Music Publications Team

To keep up–to-date with our new releases, why not
follow us on Twitter

@WMPublications

Index

Page

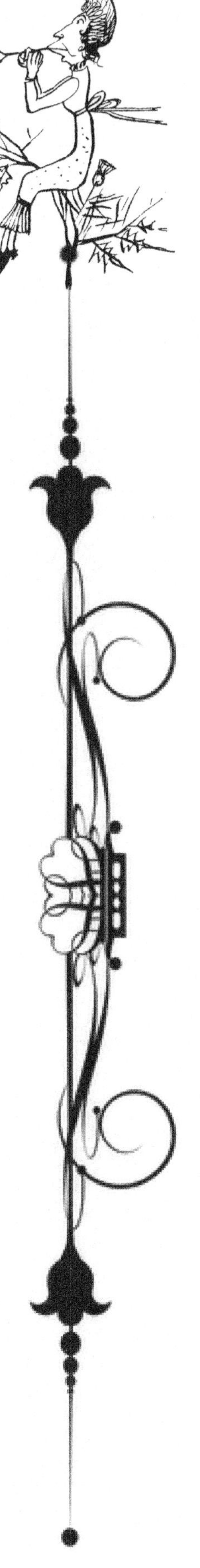

Information

Tempo and Expression Markings

Adagio – slow and stately
Alla Marcia – like a march
Allegretto – moderately fast
Allegro – fast and bright
Andante – at walking speed
Andante quasi allegretto – faster than *Andante*
Andantino – slightly faster (or sometimes slower) than *Andante*
brillante – spirited and sparkling
con moto – in a spirited manner
delicato – delicately
dolce – sweetly
giocoso – cheerful
grazioso – gracefully
Grave solemn and slow
Largamente – slow and broad
Largo – slow and stately
Lent – slow and broad
Maestoso – majestically
ma non troppo – but not too much
Moderato - moderately
in modo di marcia funebre – like a funeral march
Nicht schnell – not fast
piacevole – pleasant and agreeable
poco moto – with movement but not too fast
pomposo – pompous and stately
Presto – extremely fast
sostenuto – sustained
sotto voce – a dramatic lowering of volume
Vivace – lively and fast
Vivo – lively and brisk
a tempo – in time (or return to original speed)
accel. – *accelerando* – get gradually faster
rall. – *rallentando* – gradually slowing down
rit. – *ritenuto* – get slightly slower
ritard. – *ritardando* – get gradually slower
al fine – to the end
fermata – pause on this note

dim. – *diminuendo* – gradually softer

cresc. – *crescendo* – gradually louder
pp – *pianissimo* – very softly
p – *piano* – softly
mp – *mezzo piano* moderately soft
mf – *mezzo forte* – moderately loud
f – *forte* – loud
ff – *fortissimo* – very loud
fff *fortississimo* – very, very loud
fp – *fortepiano* – loud then immediately soft
sf – *subito forte* – suddenly loud
rf – *rinforzando* – with increasing emphasis
fz – *forzando* – forced beyond the usual dynamic for the passage
ffz – as above but stronger
sfz – *sforzando* – suddenly forced
gradually getting softer
gradually getting louder

Articulation

staccato – short and detached
leggiero – play lightly

accent – played with attack

tenuto – held– pressured accent

marcato – forcefully

Ornaments

trill – rapid movement to the note above and back or from the note above in Mozart and earlier music.

mordent – three rapid notes – the principal note, the note above and the principal.

acciaccatura – a very quick note

appoggiatura – divide the main note equally between the two notes.

Allegretto

from *Symphony No. 7 (second movement)*

Beethoven's seventh symphony was premiered in Vienna in 1813 at a charity concert for wounded soldiers. The second movement was immediately encored.
Allegretto - moderately fast but slower than *Allegro*.
pp - *pianissimo* - very soft

O sole mio

Neapolitan Song

Eduard di Capua
(1865-1917)

O sole mio - tr. 'my sun' A famous rendition was given by Pavarotti in 1980.
Andante - walking speed - fairly slow
mp - *mezzo piano* - moderately soft

Là ci darem la mano

from *Don Giovanni*

Wolfgang Amadeus Mozart
(1756-1791)

La ci darem la mano - tr. 'we will give each other our hands' is a duet between Don Giovanni and Zerlina.
Don Giovanni - an opera based on the legends of Don Juan.
Largo - slow and stately
mf - *mezzo forte* - moderately loud

Skaters' Waltz

Waltz - dance with three beats to a bar
Skaters' Waltz was inspired by the
Rink of Scaters at the Bois de Boulogne in Paris.
Allegretto - moderately fast
mp - *mezzo piano* - moderately soft
mf - *mezzo forte* - moderately loud
p - *piano* - soft

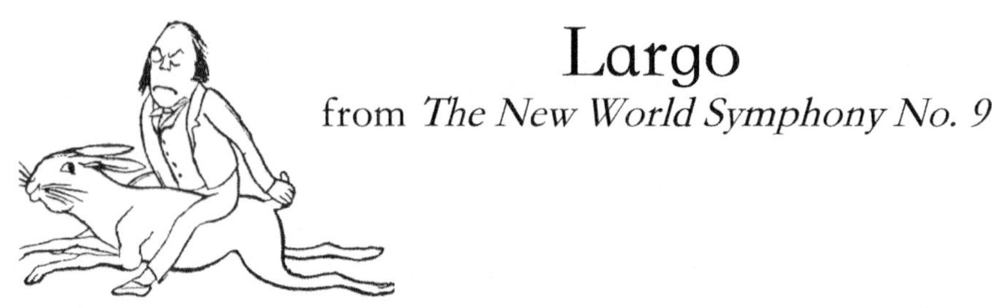

Largo

from *The New World Symphony No. 9*

Antonín Dvořák
(1841-1904)

Largo

Largo - slow and stately
Famously, Neil Armstrong took a recording of the New World Symphony on his voyage to the moon in 1969.
p - *piano* - soft
mf - *mezzo forte* - moderately loud
cresc. - *crescendo* - gradually getting louder
f *forte* - loud

Ecossaise

Ludvig van Beethoven
(1770-1827)

Moderato

1 5 9 13

1. 2.

f *mf* *p* *mf*

Ecossaise - a lively dance in Scottish style
Moderato - at a moderate speed - not too fast
f - *forte* - loud
mf - *mezzo forte* - moderately loud
p - *piano* - soft

Overture

from *The Barber of Seville*

Overture - musical introduction to an opera or play.
The Barber of Seville from the play by by Pierre Beaumarchais, revolves around the barber, Figaro, who also featured thirty years earlier in Mozart's opera, *The Marriage of Figaro.*
Allegro vivace - fast and lively
mp - *mezzo piano* - moderately soft

Minuet

Johann Sebastian Bach
(1685-1750)

Minuet - a slow stately dance
Moderato - at a moderate speed - not too fast
mf - mezzo forte - moderately loud

Humming Song

from *Album for the Young*

Robert Schumann
(1810-1856)

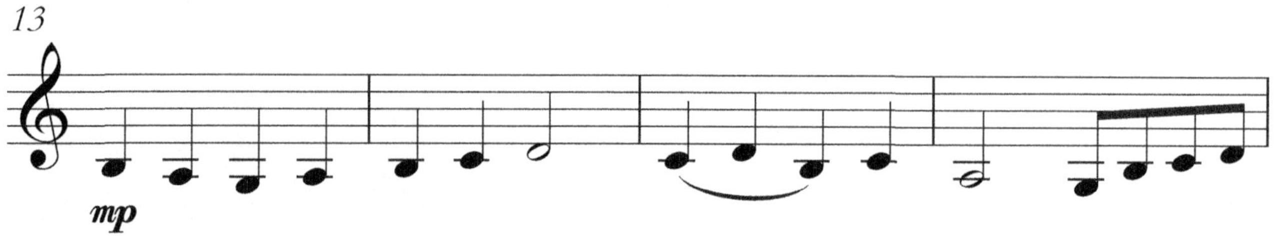

Ariette

Wolfgang Amadeus Mozart
(1756-1791)

Ariette - a song for one voice
Allegretto - moderately fast
mp - *mezzo piano* - moderately soft
mf - *mezzo forte* - moderately loud
p - *piano* - soft

Nicht schnell - not fast
mp - *mezzo piano* - moderately soft

Little Piece

from *Album for the Young*

Nicht schnell

Robert Schumann
(1810-1856)

mp

mf

5

mp

9

13

mf

Nicht schnell - not fast
mf - *mezzo forte* - moderately loud
mp - *mezzo piano* - moderately soft

Tambourin

Jean-Philippe Rameau
(1683-1764)

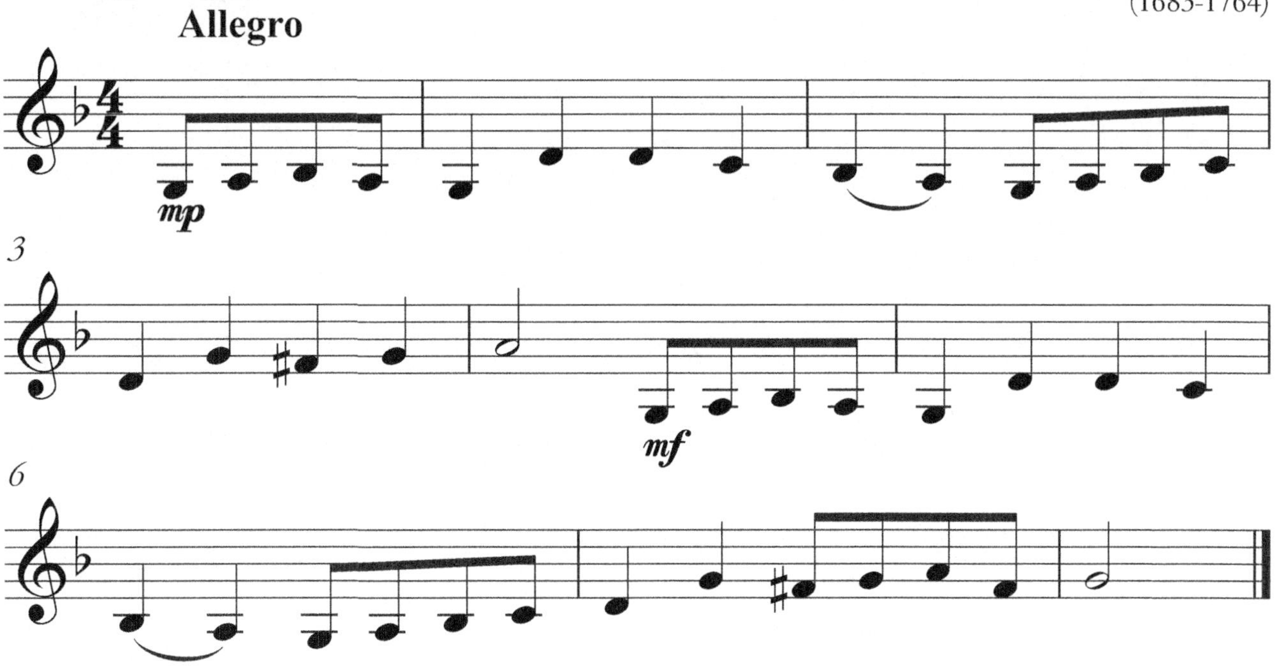

Allegro

mp

3

mf

6

Tambourin - a Provençal dance accompanied by a drum
Allegro - fast
mf - *mezzo forte* - moderately loud
mp - *mezzo piano* - moderately soft

The Anvil Chorus

from *Il Trovatore*

Giuseppe Verdi
(1813-1901)

Moderato

Il Trovatore - tr. 'The Troubadour', Verdi's opera.
The Anvil Chorus - famous song sung by gypsies in the opera.
Moderato - at a moderate speed - not too fast
f - *forte* - loud
mp - *mezzo piano* - moderately soft
mf - *mezzo forte* - moderately loud

Chaconne
from *The Fairy Queen*

Henry Purcell
(1659-1695)

The Fairy Queen - as series of short masques written by Purcell to accompany Shakespeare's play 'A Midsummer Night's Dream'.
Chaconne - originally a quick Spanish dance which later evolved into a slow instrumental piece
Andante - walking speed - fairly slow
f - *forte* - loud
mp - *mezzo piano* - moderately soft

Panis Angelicus

from *Messe a trois voix*

César Franck
(1822-1890)

Poco lento

p *f* *p*

Panis Angelicus - tr. 'bread of angels'
Poco lento - fairly slow
p - *piano* - soft
f - *forte* - loud

Prélude

from *Te Deum*

Prelude - a short musical preface.
Te Deum - a Christian hymn or service.
Moderato, alla Marcia - at a moderaste speed, like a march
mf *mezzo forte* - moderately loud
f - *forte* - loud

March

from *Scipione*

George Frideric Handel

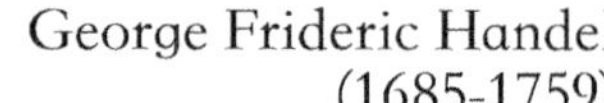

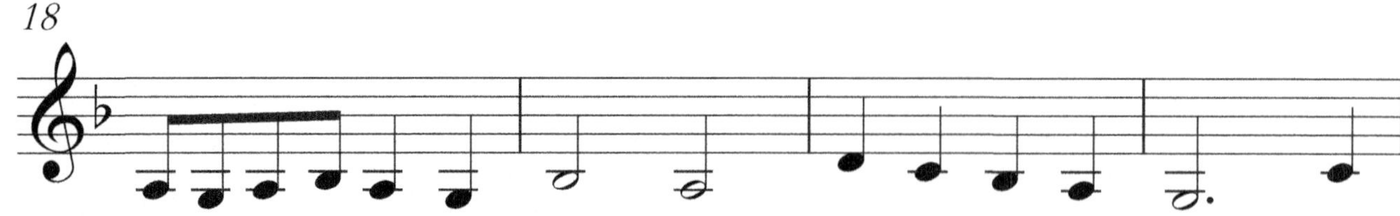

Theme

from *Symphony No. 1 Opus 68*

Johannes Brahms
(1833-1897)

Allegro con brio - fast with spirit
mf - *mezzo forte* - moderately loud

Scipione - an opera based on the life of the Roman general Scipio Africanus.
Andante maestoso - slow, with majesty
rit. - ritardando - gradually slow down
mf *mezzo forte* - moderately loud
f - *forte* - loud

Waves of the Danube

Waves of the Danube is one of the most famous Romanian tunes in the world.
Tempo di Valse - as a waltz
p - *piano* - soft
f - *forte* - loud

La Folia

from *Sonata No. 12*

Arcangelo Corelli
(1653-1713)

1 **Adagio**

p

5

9

p

13

pp

La Folia - tr. madness or folly
The *Folia* is a musical framework based on chord progressions.
Adagio - slowly
p - *piano* - soft
pp - *pianissimo* - very soft

Theme

from *Pastoral Symphony No. 6 (first movement)*

Ludvig van Beethoven
(1770-1827)

1 **Allegro**

f

5

10

14

Beethoven loved nature and spent a lot of time walking in the country. The first movement of the Pastoral symphony shows the cheerful arrival in the countryside.
Allegro - fast
f - *forte* - loud

Nessun Dorma
from *Turandot*

Giacomo Puccini
(1858-1924)

Nessun Dorma - tr. 'let no one sleep' is one of the best-known tenor arias, and was performed by José Carreras in several World Cup Finals.
Turandot - Puccini's final opera.
Andante sostenuto - moderately slow and played smoothly
mf - *mezzo forte* - moderately loud
f - *forte* - loud

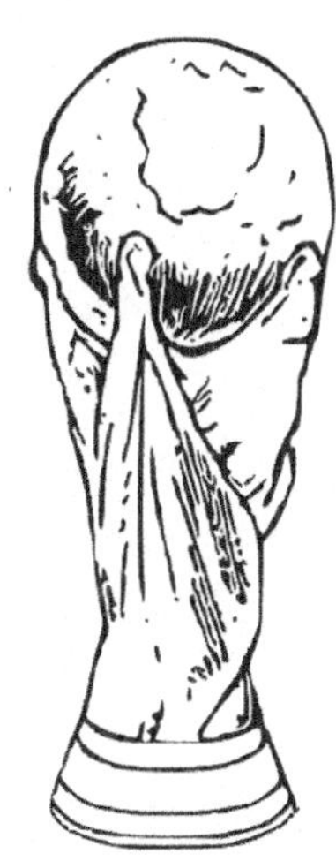

Marche Militaire

Marche Militaire - tr. 'Military March' is one of Schubert's most famous melodies.
Allegro vivace - fast and lively
p - *piano* - soft
f - *forte* - loud

Pilgrim's Chorus

from *Tannhäuser*

Richard Wagner
(1813-1883)

Andante maestoso

Tannhäuser - an opera based on German legend.
Andante maestoso - moderately slow, with majesty
p - *piano* - soft
f - *forte* - loud

Lascia ch'io pianga

from *Rinaldo*

George Frideric Handel
(1695-1759)

Larghetto

mp

mf

mp

Lascia ch'io pianga - tr. 'Leave me so that I may cry"
Larghetto - not quite as slow as Largo
mf - *mezzo forte* - moderately loud
mp - *mezzo piano* - moderately soft

La Cinquantaine

Jean Gabriel Marie
(1852-1928)

La Cinquantaine - tr. fiftieth anniversary
Andantino - relaxed, moderate tempo
mf - *mezzo forte* - moderately loud
mp - mezzo piano - moderately soft
p - *piano* - soft
f - *forte* - loud
D.S. al Fine - go back to the sign and play to Fine

Hornpipe
from *Abdelazer*

Hornpipe - a dance later associated with sailors.
Abdelazer - or *The Moor's Revenge.* Purcell wrote incidental music for the play by Aphra Behn
Allegretto - moderately fast
mf - *mezzo forte* - moderately loud
f - *forte* - loud
p - piano - soft

L'Angelus - tr. The Angel - in this case, the ringing of church bells announcing prayers.
Moderato - at a moderate speed
mf - *mezzo forte* - moderately loud
f - *forte* - loud
p - piano - soft

L'Angélus
Charles Gounod
(1818-1893)
Moderato
1
mf
4
p
7
mf
p
11
mf
14
f
18
p
21
mf

Clair de Lune

from *Suite bergamasque*

Claude Debussy
(1862-1918)

Andante tres expressif

1

pp

5

8

p

11

14

Clair de Lune - tr. Moonlight, is based on Verlaine's poem 'Clair de lune'.
Suite Bergamasque - Debussy's piano suite refers to a bergamaska, a rustic dance originating in Bergano, Italy.
Andante tres expressif - at a moderate pace, with great expression
pp - pianissimo - very soft
p - piano - soft

Theme

from *Piano Concerto No. 1*

Pyotr Ilyich Tchaikovsky
(1840-1893)

Andante

f

4

8

12

15

p

The *Piano Concerto No. 1* by Tchaikovsky is among the best known of all piano concertos.
Andante - at a moderate speed
mf - *mezzo forte* - moderately loud
f - *forte* - loud
p - piano - soft

Theme

from *Danse Macabre*

Camille Saint-Saëns
(1835-1921)

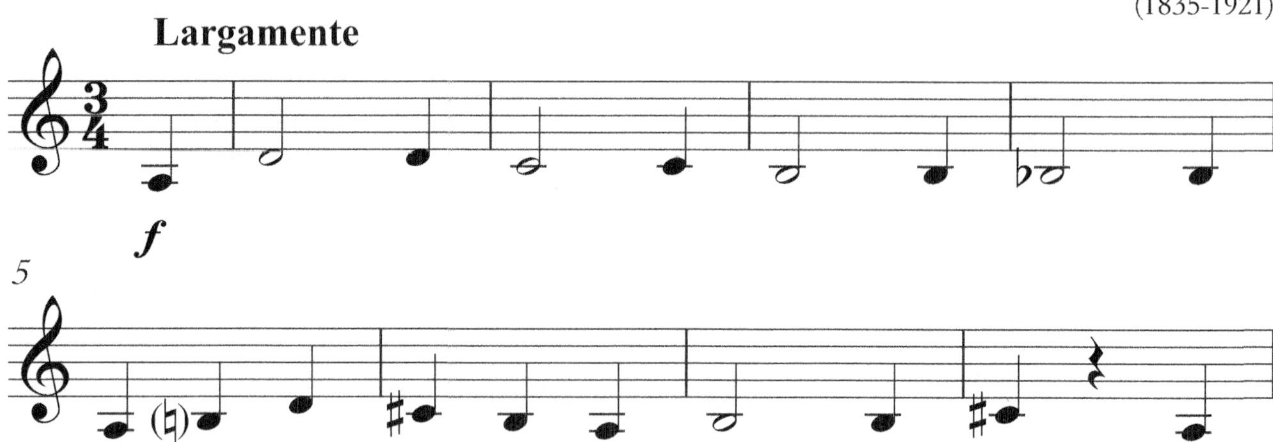

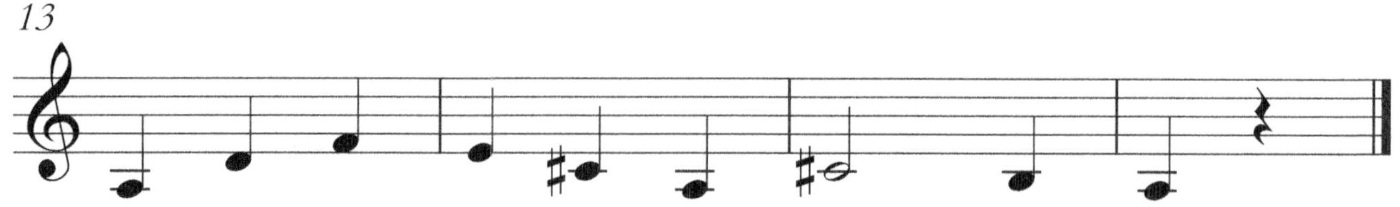

Danse Macabre - tr. 'Dance of Death', a tone poem for orchestra set on Halloween.
Largamente - slow and broad
f - *forte* - loud

Garland Waltz
from *Sleeping Beauty*

Pyotr Ilyich Tchaikovsky
(1840-1893)

Waltz - a dance with three beats in a bar.
Sleeping Beauty - a ballet based on the fairy tale,
Allegro - fast
mf - *mezzo forte* - moderately loud
f - *forte* - loud

The Sorcerer's Apprentice

Paul Dukas
(1865-1935)

Allegro

1

mp

7

13

19

25

The Sorcerer's Apprentice - a symphonic poem appearing in Disney's *Fantasia* and inspired by Goethe's ballad.
Allegro - fast.
mp - mezzo piano - moderately soft

Boléro

Maurice Ravel
(1875-1937)

Bolero - a slow ballroom dance originating in Spain. Ravel's Bolero is a one movement ballet for orchestra. The melody is adapted from a Sufi melody.
Moderato - at a moderate speed
pp - pianissimo - very soft
mp - mezzo piano - moderately soft
mf - mezzo *forte* - moderately loud

The Aquarium

from *Carnival of the Animals*

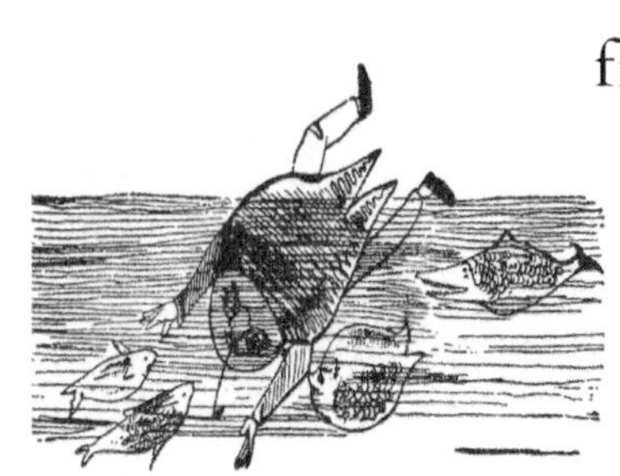

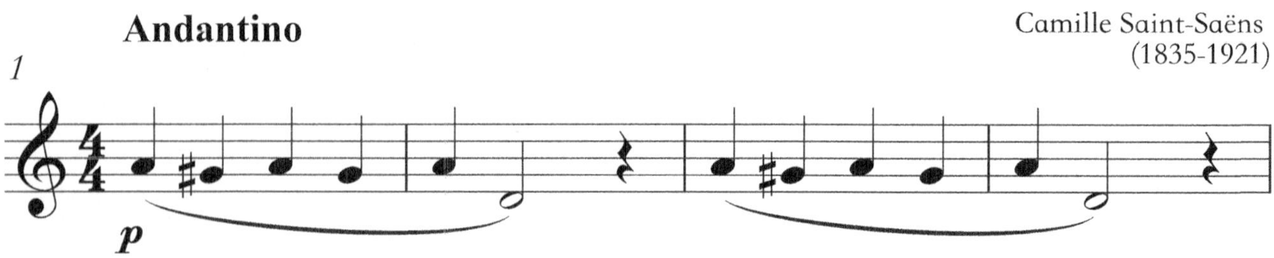

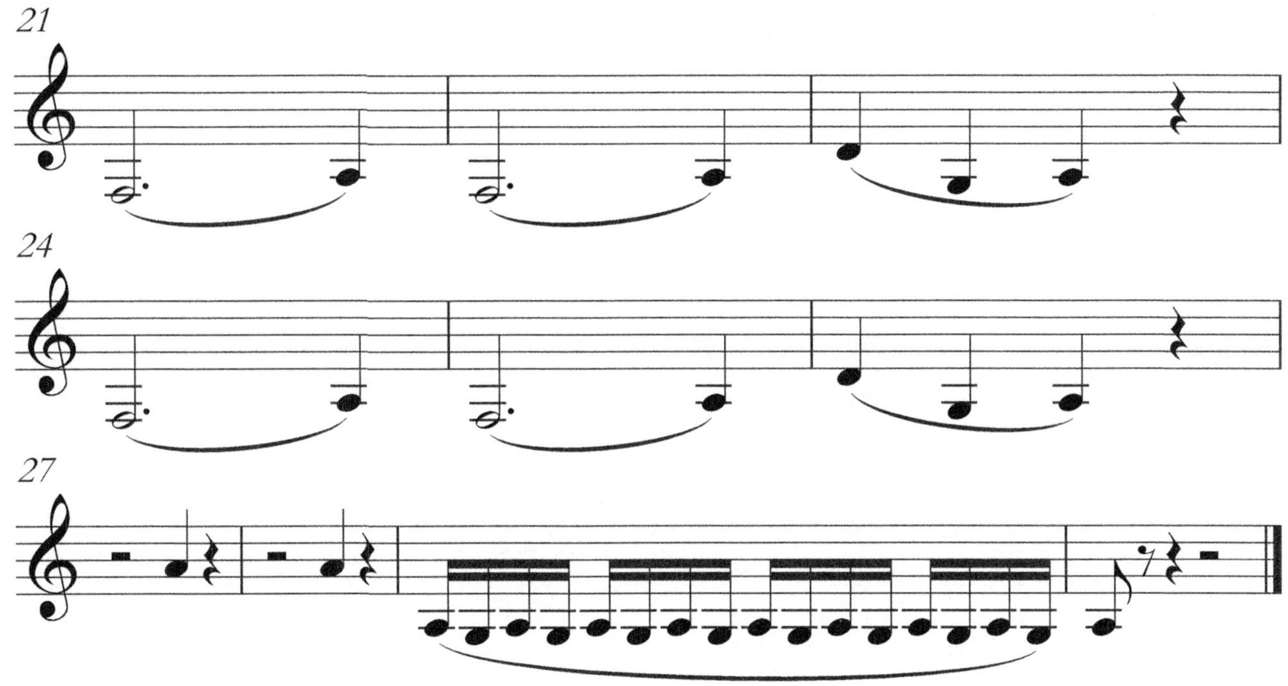

Carnival of the Animals - a humorous orchestral suite of fourteen movements.
The Aquarium - scored for strings, two pianos, flute and glass harmonica.
Andantino - a relaxed moderate tempo, slightly slower than *Andante*.
p - piano - soft

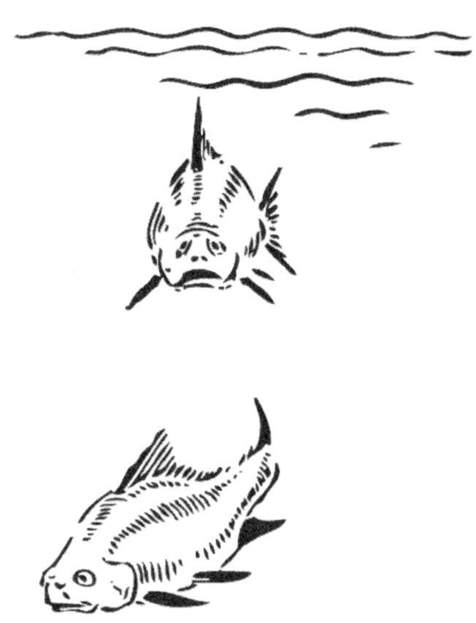

Marche Slave

Opus 31

Je crois entendre encore - tr. 'I still believe I hear'.
The Pearl Fishers - an opera set in ancient Ceylon
Andante - moderately slow
sempre legato - smoothly throughout
pp - *pianissimo* - very soft
mf - *mezzo forte* - moderately loud

Marche Slave - or 'Slavic March', an orchestral tone poem written to benefit wounded Serbian soldiers.
Moderato in modo di marcia funebre - tr. at a moderate speed in the manner of a funeral march.
pp - *pianissimo* - very soft
espress. - espressivo - play expressively

Je crois entendre encore

from *The Pearl Fishers*

Georges Bizet
(1838-1875)

Andante

p

sempre legato

6

12

mf

p

18

24

p

29

pp

34

Winter

from *The Four Seasons*

Antonio Vivaldi
(1678-1741)

1 **Largo**

mf

5

9

13

The Four Seasons - four violin concerti each representing a different season, and each composed with an accompanying sonnet.
Largo - slow and stately
mf - mezzo forte - moderately loud

We tread the icy path slowly and cautiously,
for fear of tripping and falling.
Then turn abruptly, slip, crash on the ground and,
rising, hasten on across the ice lest it cracks up.
We feel the chill north winds course through the home
despite the locked and bolted doors...
this is winter, which nonetheless
brings its own delights.

La Réjouissance

from *Music for the Royal Fireworks*

George Frideric Handel
(1685-1759)

La Rejouissance - tr. 'the rejoicing'
Music for the Royal Fireworks is a suite for wind celebrating the War of Austrian Succession and performed in London's Green Park in 1749
Allegretto - moderately fast
mf - *mezzo forte* - moderately loud

Rigaudon

Henry Purcell
(1659-1695)

Rigaudon - a lively baroque dance originating in France.
Allegretto - moderately fast
mp - *mezzo piano* - moderately soft
mf - *mezzo forte* - moderately loud
f - *forte* - loud

Amami, Alfredo

from *La Traviata*

Giuseppe Verdi
(1813-1901)

Amami, Alfredo - tr. 'Love me, Alfredo'
La Traviata - an opera based on Alexandre Dumas' novel 'La Dame aux camélias'.
Adagio - slow
con passione e forza - with passion and strength
ff - *fortissimo* - very loud
p - *piano* - soft

Romance

Fernando Sor
(1778-1839)

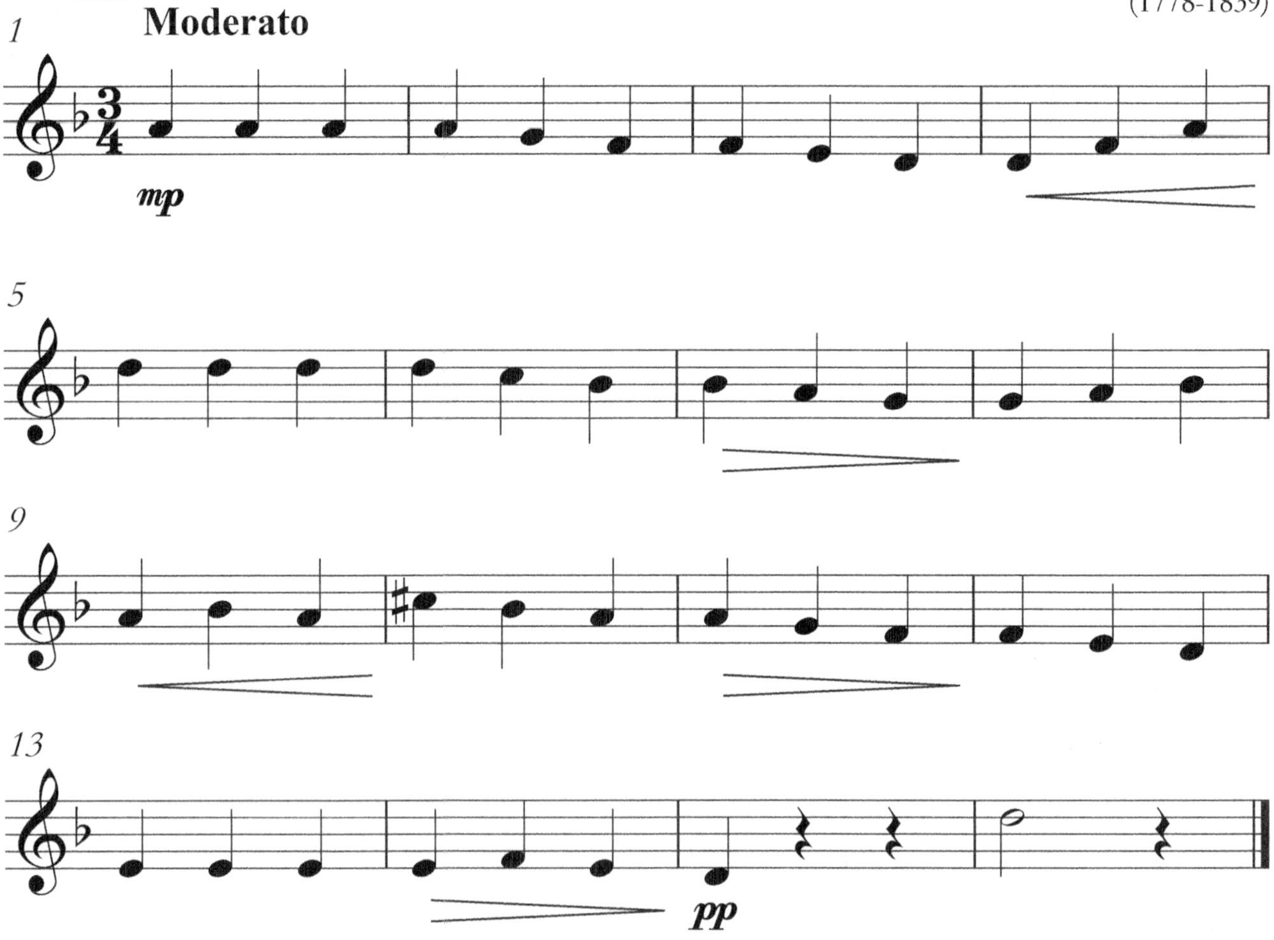

1 **Moderato**

mp

5

9

13

pp

Romance was originaly written for guitar and is an example of Spanish parlour music.
Moderato - at a moderate speed
mp - *mezzo piano* - moderately soft
pp - pianissimo - very soft

Gavotte

François-Joseph Gossec
(1840-1893)

Gavotte - a lively French dance.
Allegretto - moderately fast
p - *piano* - soft
mf - *mezzo forte* - moderately loud

Tales from the Vienna Woods

Opus 325

Johann Strauss
(1825-1899)

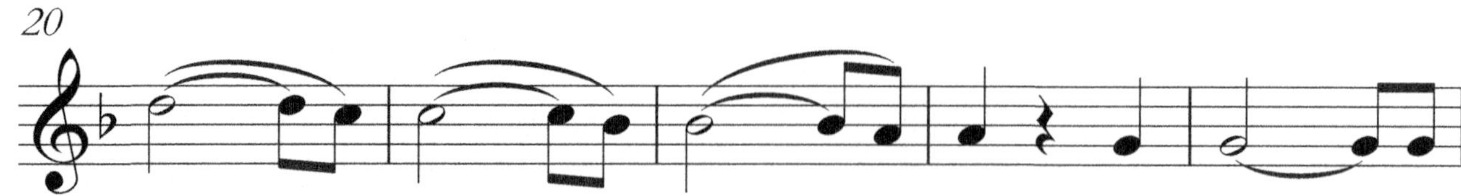

Tales of the Vienna Woods - is one of six waltzes featuring a virtuoso zither part. The title refers to the folk music of the inhabitants of the woods.
Vivo - lively and animated
mf - mezzo forte - moderately loud

Waltz

from *Danse Macabre*

Camille Saint-Saëns
(1835-1921)

Waltz - a dance with three beats in a bar
Danse Macabre - tr. 'Dance of Death', a tone poem for orchestra set on Halloween.
Moderato - at a moderate speed
f - *forte* - loud
p - *piano* - soft

Romanze
from *Eine Kleine Nachtmusik*

Wolfgang Amadeus Mozart
(1756-1791)

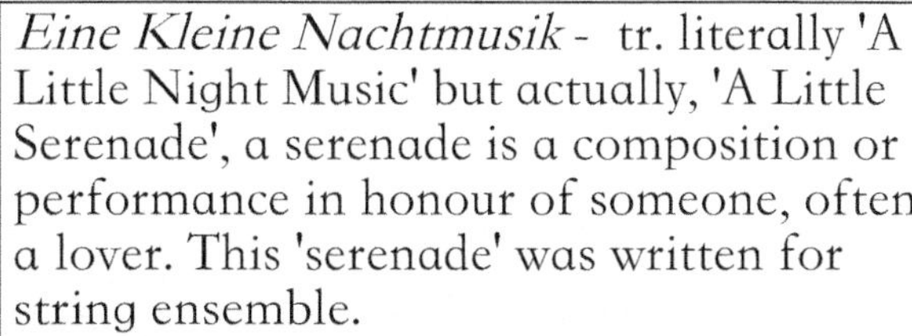
Eine Kleine Nachtmusik - tr. literally 'A Little Night Music' but actually, 'A Little Serenade', a serenade is a composition or performance in honour of someone, often a lover. This 'serenade' was written for string ensemble.
Andante - moderately slow
p - piano - soft
f - *forte* - loud

1812 Overture

Pyotr Ilyich Tchaikovsky
(1840-1893)

1812 Overture - a festival overture for orchestra written to commemorate the successful Russian defence against Napoleon's invading army, famous for its volley of cannon fire.
Allegro vivace - fast and lively
f - *forte* - loud

Dance of the Cygnets

from *Swan Lake*

Pyotr Ilyich Tchaikovsky
(1840-1893)

1 **Allegro moderato**

mp

4

7

p

10

13

p

15

Dance of the Cygnets - a dance for four unison ballerinas.
Swan Lake - ballet based on Russian and German folk tales.
Allegro moderato - moderately fast
mp - *mezzo piano* - moderately soft
p - *piano* - soft

Funeral March of a Marionette

from *Suite Burlesque*

Funeral March of a Marionette - an orchestral piece based on the story of a marionette who has died in a duel.
Allegretto - moderately fast
p - *piano - soft*
f - *forte* - loud

Gnossienne 1

Erik Satie
(1866-1925)

Gnossienne - (a word invented by Satie) - experimental pieces written for piano
Lent - slow and broad
p - piano - soft
f - forte - loud

Fossils

from *Carnival of the Animals*

Camille Saint-Saëns
(1835-1921)

Allegro ridicolo

Carnival of the Animals - a humorous orchestral suite of fourteen movements.
Fossils - mimicking *Danse macabre* with xylophone solo, and allusions to 'Twinkle Twinkle Little Star' and 'Au clair de la lune'.
Allegro ridicolo - fast and ridiculous
mp - mezzo piano - moderately soft
ff - fortissimo - very loud
p - piano - soft

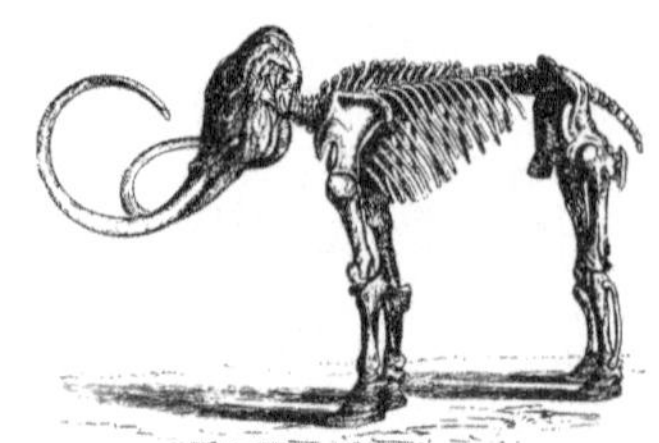

Scheherazade

from *Suite Symphonique Op. 35*

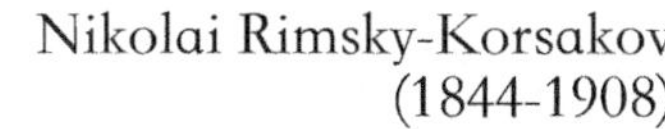

Scheherazade - an orchestral suite based on the stories 'One Thousand and One Nights'. Sheherazade is the female storyteller.
Andantino quasi allegretto - a relaxed moderate tempo but not too slow.
p - piano - soft

Bagatelle 2
from *Seven Bagatelles*

Scherzo
Allegro

Ludvig van Beethoven
(1770-1827)

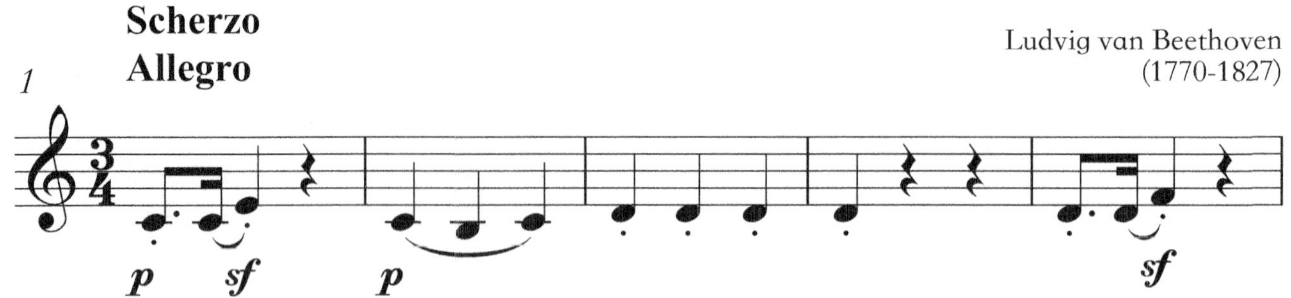

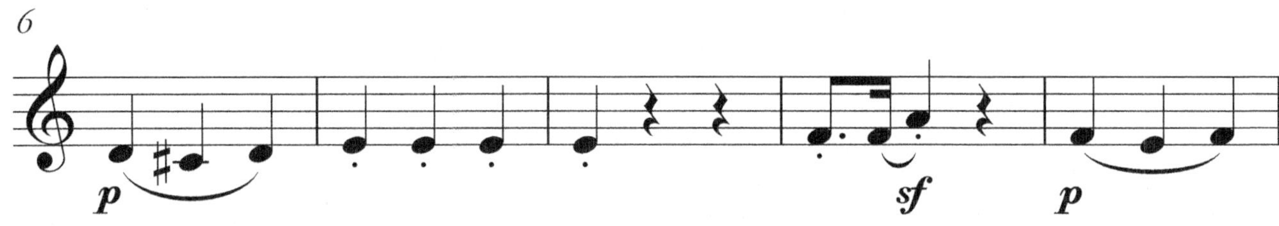

Bagatelle - a light unpretentious piece of music.
Beethoven's *Bagatelles* were written for piano.
Scherzo - playful
Allegro - fast
Minore - indicates a section in a minor key.
p - piano - soft
sf - subito forte - suddenly loud
ff - fortissimo - very loud
D.C. al Fine - Da Capo al Fine - go back to the beginning and play to *Fine.*

Duetto Buffo di Due Gatti

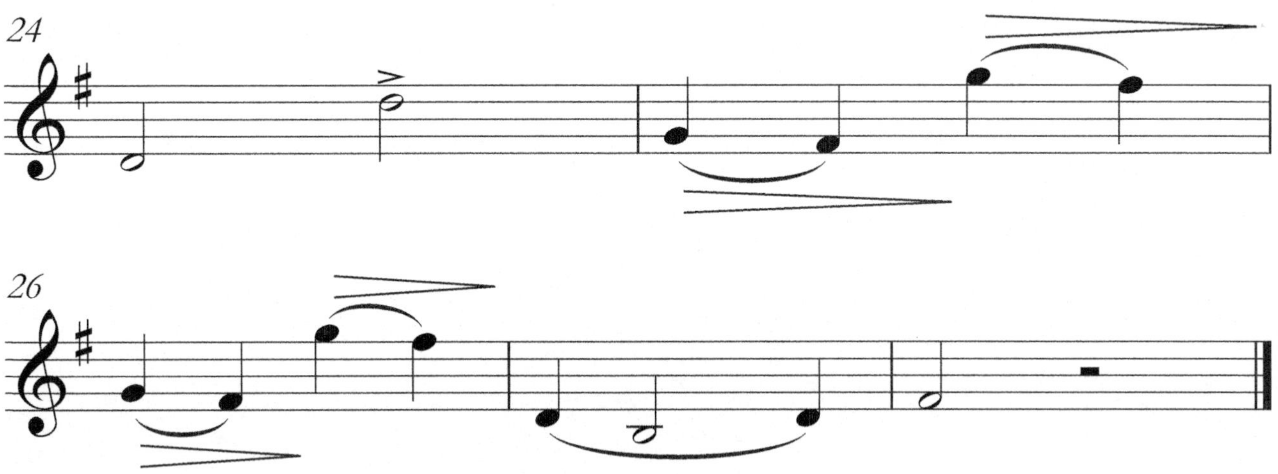

Duetto Buffo di Due Gatti - tr. 'humorous duet for two cats'. Popular performance piece for two sopranos in which the lyrics consist entirely of the word 'meow'.
Adagio - slow
sempre legato - play smoothly throughout the piece.
p - piano - soft

Carol of the Bells

Ukranian Bell Carol

Mykola Leontovych
(1877-1921)

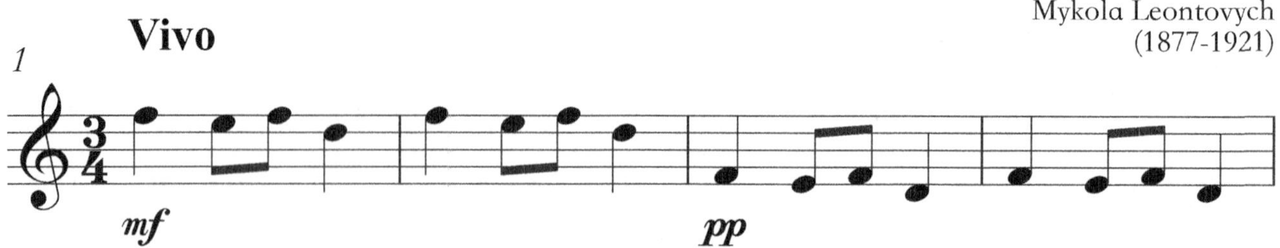

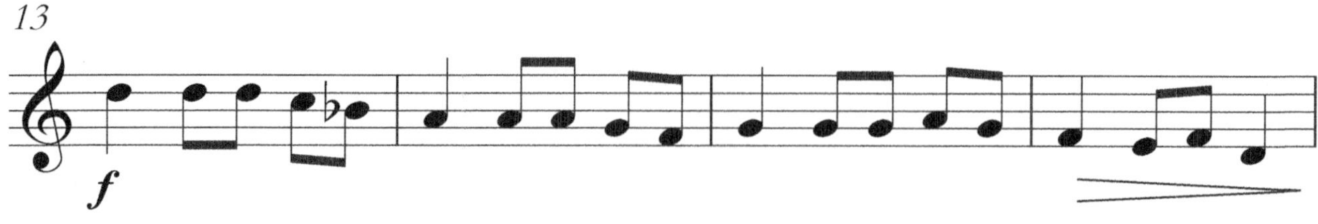

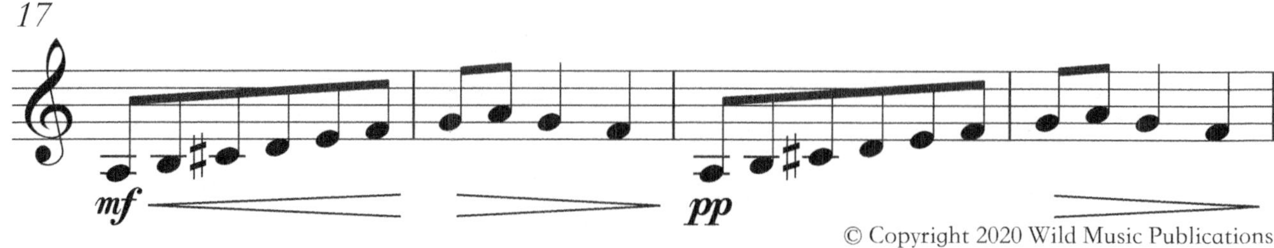

Carol of the Bells - a choral piece based on Ukranian folk chants, sung at New Year and telling of a swallow who flies into the house to proclaim the bountiful year that the family will have.
Vivo - lively and brisk
mf - mezzo forte - moderately loud
pp - pianissimo - very soft
f - forte - loud
mp - mezzo piano - moderately soft
rit. - ritardando - gradually slower

Adagio Cantabile

from *Piano Sonata No. 8 'Pathetique'*

Ludvig van Beethoven
(1770-1827)

Pathetique - called 'Pathetique' because of the tragic and expressive nature of the piece.
Adagio cantabile - slowly, in a singing style
p - *piano* - soft
sf - *subito forte* - suddenly loud
fp - *fortepiano* - loud then immediately soft
pp - *pianissimo* - very soft

Funiculì, funiculà

Luigi Denza
(1846-1922)

Allegro brillante

Funiculì, funiculà - song composed to commemorate the opening of the first funicular railway on Mount Vesuvius. *Allegro brillante* - fast, showy and spirited *f* - *forte* - loud *p* - *piano* - soft *pp* - *pianissimo* - very soft

Étude - *Tristesse*

Opus 10 No. 3

Frédéric Chopin
(1810-1849)

Lento ma non troppo

Étude - tr. 'Study' - a technical piece designed to develop instrumental technique. Chopin's *Études* were revolutionary in piano playing style, and the Opus 10 were written while he was still in his teens.
Tristesse - tr. 'Sadness'
Lento ma non troppo - slowly but not too much so
poco accel. - *poco accelerando* - get a little faster
rit. - *ritardando.* - gradually slower
A tempo. - tr. 'in time' - resume original speed
p - *piano* - soft
f - *forte* - *loud*
pp - *pianissimo* - very soft

Colonel Bogey March

Kenneth J. Alford
(1881-1945)

Quick March

1 *f*

5 *p*

9

13

17 *mf*

21 *mf*

25

Colonel Bogey March was written by Kenneth J. Alford, alias Major F. J. Ricketts, a British army bandmaster who became director of the Royal Marines. He used a pen name because, at the time, it was frowned upon for commissioned officers to be engaged in commercial activities.
Colonel Bogey was inspired by golfers whistling while playing in Scotland.
f - *forte* - loud

Hallelujah Chorus

from *Messiah*

George Frideric Handel
(1685-1759)

Messiah - an oratorio, and one of the best know choral works in Western music.
Allegro - fast
f - *forte* - loud

Glossary of Musical Terms

Here are commonly used musical terms. If you wish to discover more detailed Music Theory, try our Flute theory book, The Flying Flute Music Theory Book 1.

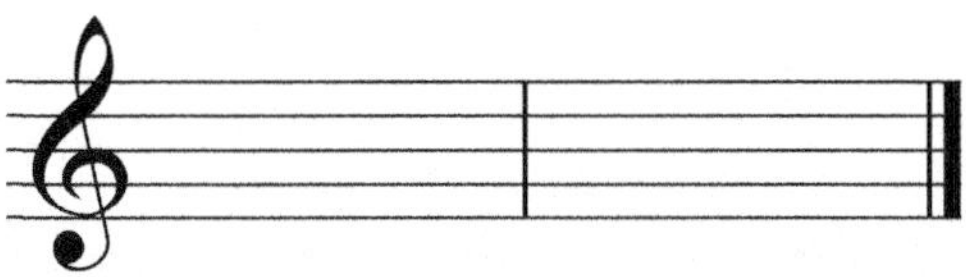

Staff or Stave
The 5 lines on which music is written.

Bars and Bar Lines
Music is divided into bars by barlines.

The end of a piece is shown by a thin line and a thick line.

- Semibreve - Four beats
- Dotted Minim - Three beats
- Minim - Two beats
- Dotted Crotchet - One and a half beats
- Crotchet - One beat
- Two Quavers - One crotchet beat
- Quaver - One half beat
- . A dot next to a note adds on half of the value of that note

Treble Clef - found at the start of a stave and showing high sounding instruments.

Semibreve rest - Four beats silence

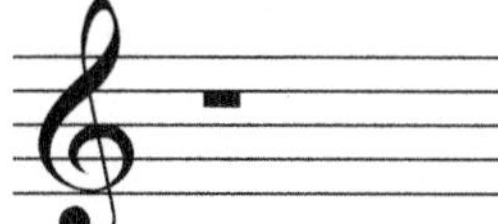

Minim rest - Two beats silence

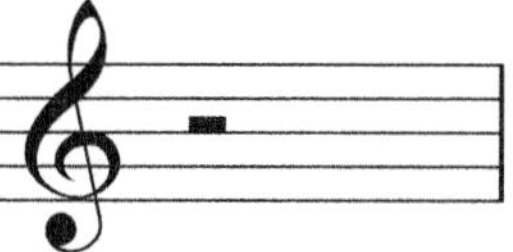

Crotchet rest - One beat silence

Repeat Sign - Play again either from the beginning or from the facing repeat sign.

Slur - a loop joing notes of different pitch - tongue the first note and continue blowing whilst moving to the next note.

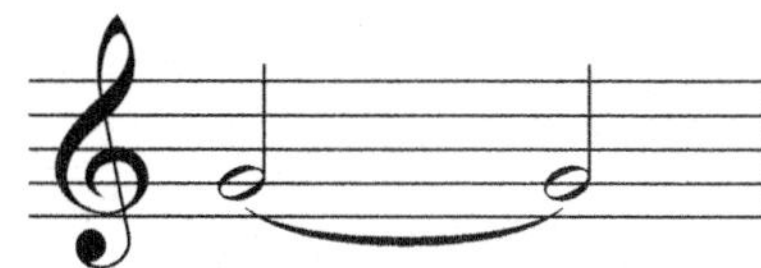

Tie - a loop joing notes that are the same pitch -join the notes together without breaking.

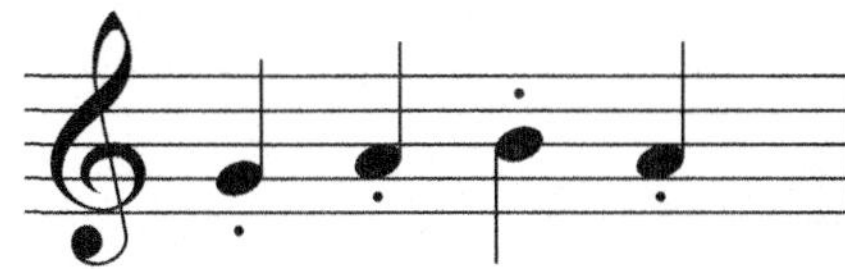

Staccato - a dot above or below a note - tongued short and detached, with a bounce.

Fermata - hold this note longer than its written value.

♯ **Sharp** - Raises a note by a semitone (half step).

♭ **Flat** - Lowers a note by a semitone (half step).

♮ **Natural** - Cancels a sharp or flat.

Key Signatures

Show which sharps or flats should be played.

One sharp means all the Fs are played F sharp.

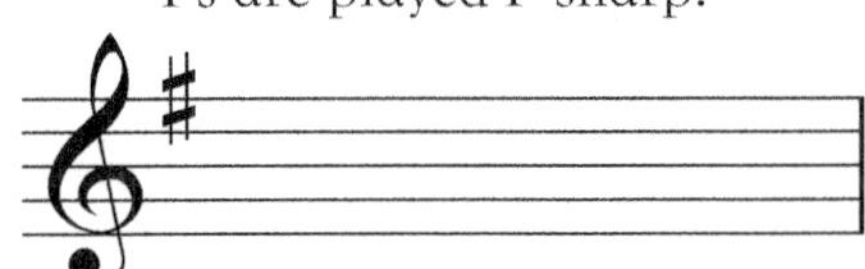

One flat means all the Bs are played B flat.

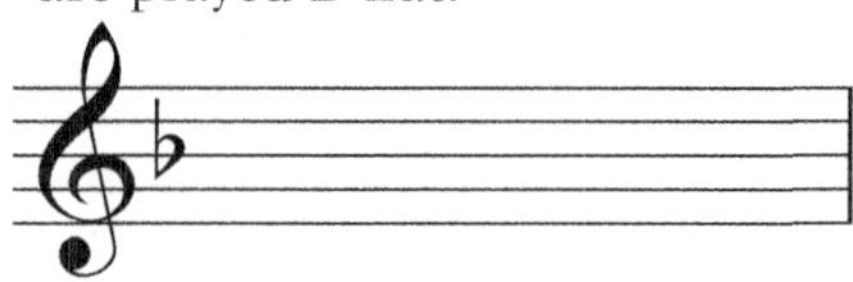

Time Signatures -

The top number shows how many beats are in a bar.
The bottom number shows what sort of beats - 4 for crotchets, 2 for minims.

Two crotchets in a bar.

Three crotchets in a bar.

Four crotchets in a bar.

Five crotchets in a bar.

Three minim beats in a bar.

Dynamics

Italian terms and abbreviations are used to show how loudly and softly we should play.

pianissimo very soft	*piano* soft	*mezzo piano* moderately soft	*mezzo forte* moderately loud	*forte* loud	*fortissimo* very loud	*crescendo* gradually louder
pp	***p***	***mp***	***mf***	***f***	***ff***	cresc.

crescendo get gradually louder

diminuendo get gradually softer

Note Recognition

Notes are named after the first seven letters of the alphabet.

Notes in the spaces spell FACE.

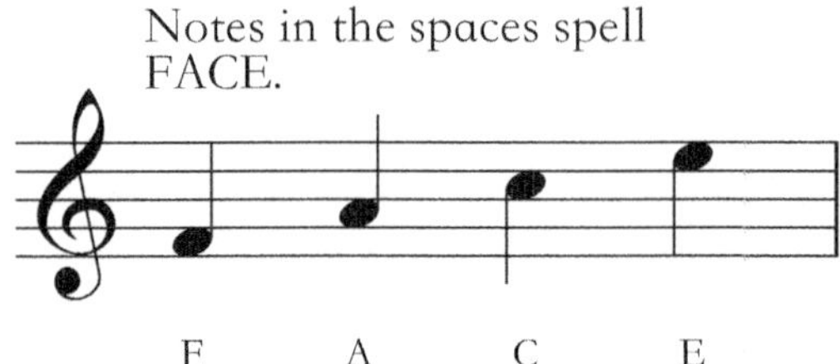

F A C E

Notes on the lines: Every Green Bus Drives Fast.

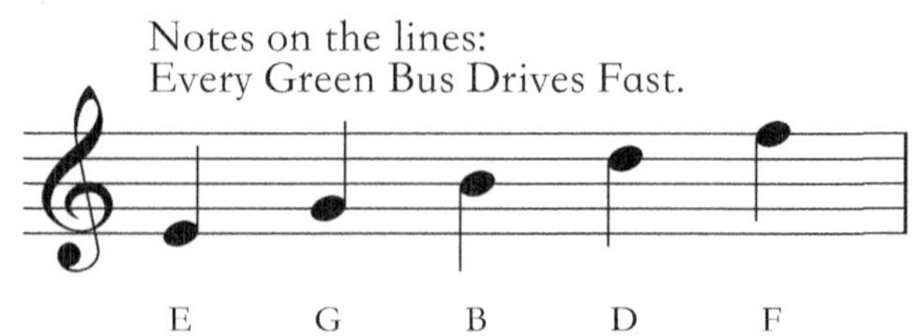

E G B D F

Ledger Lines - small lines above or below the stave on which notes are written to extend the stave to include higher or lower notes.

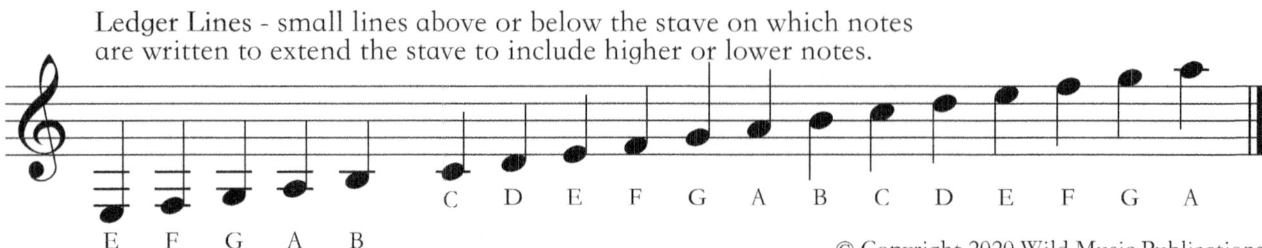

C D E F G A B C D E F G A

E F G A B

If you have enjoyed this book why not try other Catchy Clarinet books: Introducing:

Look out for more exciting clarinet music and many duet combinations at **wildmusicpublications.com**

@wmpublications

Printed in Great Britain
by Amazon